BURIED IN RUBBLE

TRUE STORIES OF SURVIVING EARTHQUAKES

BY TERRY COLLINS ILLUSTRATED BY MACK CHATER

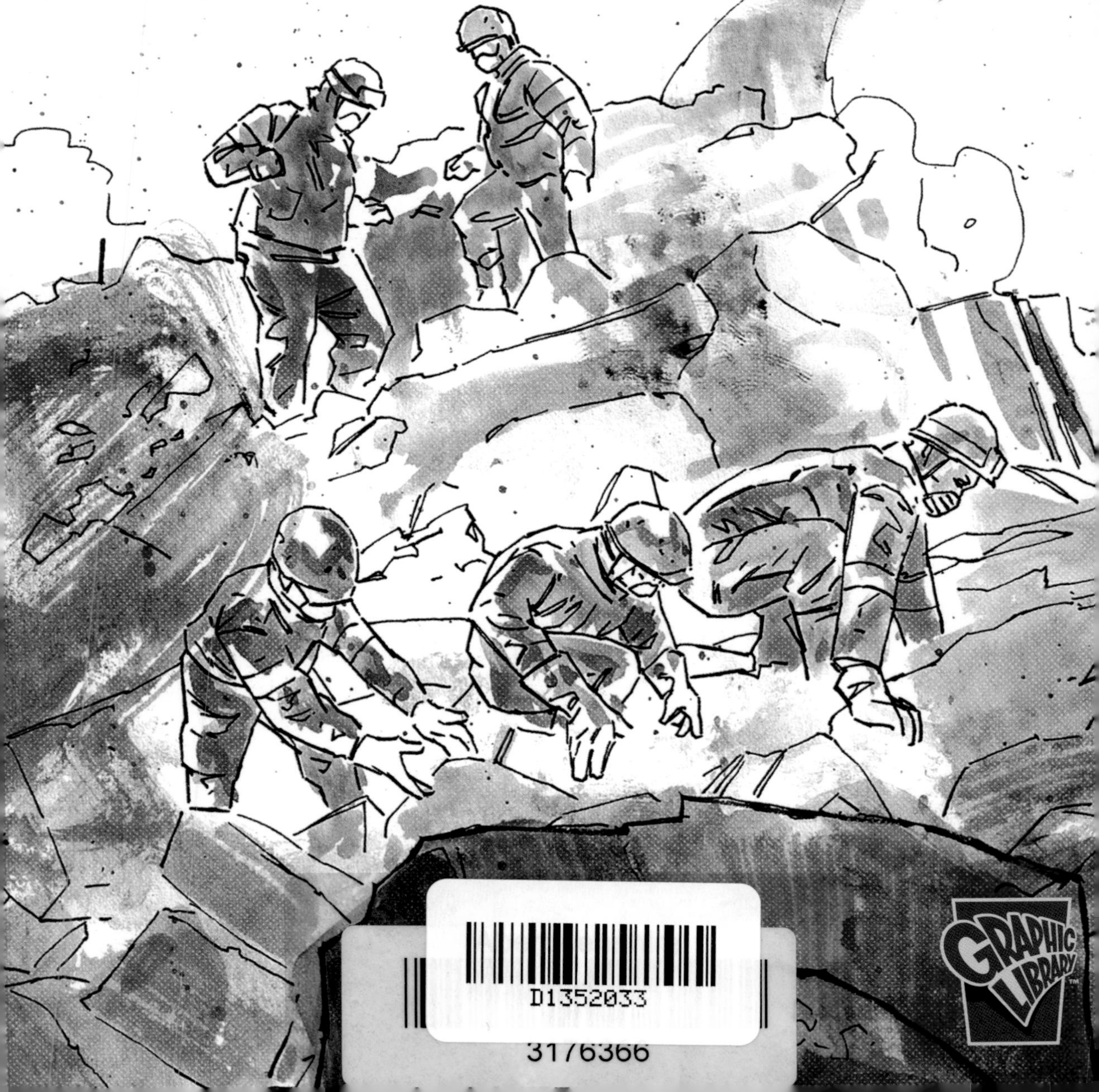

GRAPHIC LIBRARY™

Raintree is an imprint of Capstone Global Library Limited, a company incorporated in England and Wales having its registered office at 7 Pilgrim Street, London, EC4V 6LB – Registered company number: 6695582

www.raintree.co.uk
myorders@raintree.co.uk

Text © Capstone Global Library Limited 2016
The moral rights of the proprietor have been asserted.

Editorial Credits

Anthony Wacholtz. editor; Ashlee Suker, designer; Nathan Gassman, creative director; Laura Manthe, production specialist

ISBN 978 1 4747 0569 1
19 18 17 16 15
10 9 8 7 6 5 4 3 2 1

British Library Cataloguing in Publication Data

A full catalogue record for this book is available from the British Library

Every effort has been made to contact copyright holders of material reproduced in this book. Any omissions will be rectified in subsequent printings if notice is given to the publisher.

All the Internet addresses (URLs) given in this book were valid at the time of going to press. However, due to the dynamic nature of the Internet, some addresses may have changed, or sites may have changed or ceased to exist since publication. While the author and publisher regret any inconvenience this may cause readers, no responsibility for any such changes can be accepted by either the author or the publisher.

Editor's note:
Direct quotations, noted in orange type, appear on the following pages:

Page 9: http://ajw.asahi.com/article/behind_news/social_affairs/AJ201307130016

Page 11, panel 2: http://news.bbc.co.uk/2/hi/middle_east/3366571.stm

Page 11, panel 4: www.smh.com.au/articles/2004/01/04/1073151197480.html?from=storyrhs

Page 17: http://china.org.cn/china/wenchuan_earthquake/2008-05/15/content_15259200.htm

Page 20: www.telegraph.co.uk/news/worldnews/centralamericaandthecaribbean/haiti/7530686/Buried-for-27-days-Haiti-earthquake-survivors-amazing-story.html

Page 24: http://www.nzherald.co.nz/nz/news/article.cfm?c_id=1&objectid=10709233

Printed in China.

CONTENTS

NATURE'S DESTRUCTIVE FORCE: EARTHQUAKES

Earth's crust cracks open with terrific force. A chasm emerges that is large enough to swallow up parts of roads and entire homes. People take cover as buildings topple down around them.

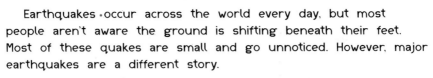

Earthquakes occur across the world every day, but most people aren't aware the ground is shifting beneath their feet. Most of these quakes are small and go unnoticed. However, major earthquakes are a different story.

The damage an earthquake can do depends on where it occurs. In cities, buildings collapse in on themselves or crumble into the streets. An earthquake can cause landslides in mountainous areas. An earthquake under the sea can create giant waves known as tsunamis. These waves can destroy beaches, property and coastlines.

In the aftermath of a major earthquake, survival is often a race against the clock. When buildings collapse, victims pinned under rubble are trapped without food or water. They may be left in the dark if the electricity is cut off. The survivor now has to stay alive long enough for help to arrive, which might take hours or even days.

The men and women in these true tales stayed calm and kept an awareness of their surroundings. They refused to give up. They lived to share their courageous stories.

CHAPTER ONE

G.A. CAIN
THE GREAT KANTO EARTHQUAKE

G.A. Cain, originally from the UK, lived and worked in Yokohama, Japan, for an insurance company. Little is known about her life other than an amazing nine-page letter she wrote about her experiences during the Great Kanto Earthquake of 1923.

1 SEPTEMBER 1923: YOKOHAMA, JAPAN

Do you want me to bring you back anything, Ms Cain?

No, thank you. I'm going home to eat today.

I'll be right back. My driver is outside and ... ohh!

RRRRRUMBLE!

At 11.58 a.m., a 7.9-magnitude earthquake struck.

The roar of falling buildings surrounded Cain and her colleagues. The room became as dark as night. The dust made it hard to breathe and see.

Is anybody hurt? We've got to get out. Aftershocks may bring the roof down on us!

Their room was the only one in the entire building not destroyed.

This way!

Be careful. Try not to cut yourself on the glass.

What Cain saw outside was unbelievable.

The quake had reduced the city of Yokohama to rubble in just two minutes. The group ran to a nearby bank. But after several aftershocks, Cain's chauffeur suggested they go to an open space.

The group of colleagues headed to Yokohama Park. Broken water mains flooded some areas. They either climbed over broken concrete and brick or waded through dirty water up to their knees.

Once they arrived, they realized that the park was not safe either. Fires burned on all sides.

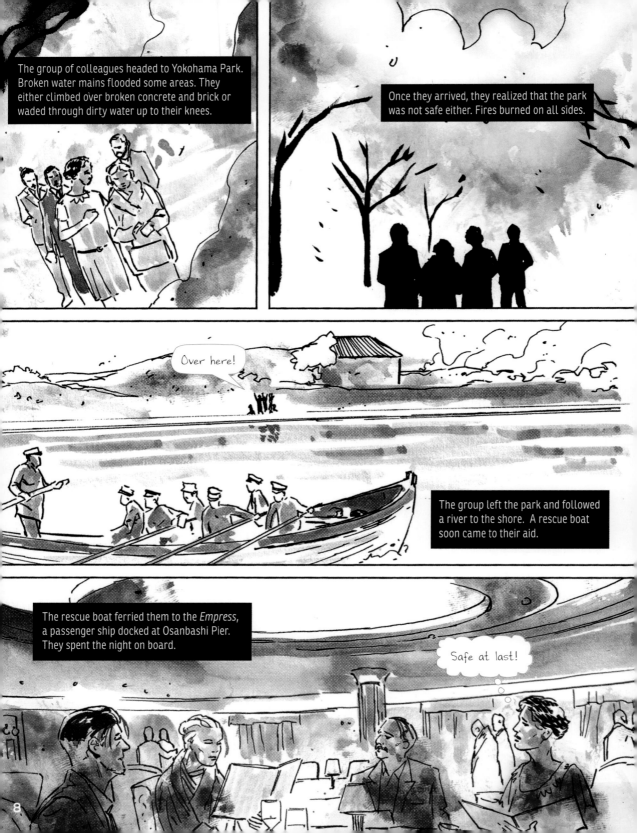

Over here!

The group left the park and followed a river to the shore. A rescue boat soon came to their aid.

The rescue boat ferried them to the *Empress*, a passenger ship docked at Osanbashi Pier. They spent the night on board.

Safe at last!

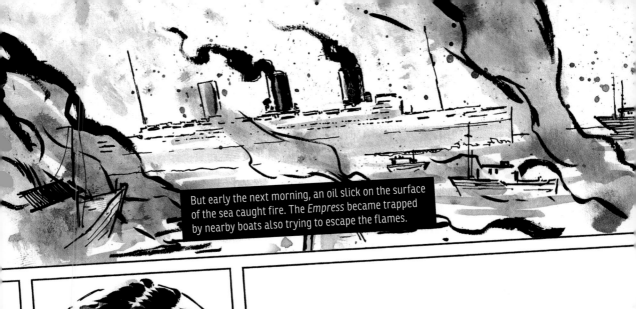

But early the next morning, an oil slick on the surface of the sea caught fire. The *Empress* became trapped by nearby boats also trying to escape the flames.

For a heartbeat, Cain thought about leaping overboard.

But before she gave up hope, the *Empress* found an opening. It slowly moved out to sea, away from the fire.

Cain later wrote about the experience: Of course you have all been hearing terrible things of what has happened to Yokohama and Tokyo. ... The wonder of it is that so many of us escaped alive.

CHAPTER TWO

SHAHR-BANU MAZANDARANI
UNLIKELY SURVIVOR

On 26 December 2003, Shahr-Banu Mazandarani, an elderly woman in Bam, Iran, had no idea her bedroom was about to become a prison.

A massive earthquake struck early in the morning. Across south-eastern Iran, an estimated 30,000 people were killed. Ninety per cent of the buildings in the historical city of Bam were either damaged or destroyed.

The search for survivors was a long and difficult task. But eight days after the tremor, rescue workers still held out hope they would find people alive.

Over here!

At first, rescuers thought the hand belonged to a corpse. Then they heard a weak voice crying out from under the rubble.

Help me.

After three hours of digging through debris, workers found Shahr-Banu Mazandarani wrapped in a blanket on her bed. Amazingly, fallen beams and furniture had protected her. Weak but alive, she asked for something to drink.

When a cup of tea was offered, she still had enough spark to scold her rescuers.

It's hot. Don't give it to me now.

How old do you think she is?

I'm not sure, but I would guess in her nineties. I can't believe she survived.

Mazandarani recovered in the hospital. When asked about how she survived, her answer was simple:

God kept me alive.

CHAPTER THREE

BRANT WEBB, TODD RUSSELL AND LARRY KNIGHT
BEACONSFIELD MINE

On 25 April 2006, 17 Australians working at the Beaconsfield Mine in Tasmania began their night shift just like any other. Little did they know the story of three men – Brant Webb, Todd Russell and Larry Knight – was about to captivate the entire nation of Australia.

The three-man crew was in a tunnel 914 metres below the mine. Russell and Webb worked in a protective cage the miners called "the basket".

The basket extended from the telehandler, a machine used for underground mining. Knight was at the controls of the telehandler.

Before they could react, the ceiling fell in on top of them.

Unable to move, the trapped men waited for help to arrive.

Good thing we were in the basket or we would have been crushed.

<cough> But what about Larry? Can you hear me, Larry?

The calls to their colleague were met with eerie silence. Without the protection of the basket, Knight had died instantly in the quake.

Meanwhile, above ground, authorities were told about the plight of the three missing miners.

Freeing the trapped miners proved to be delicate work. Great care was required in order to protect the rescuers and the victims. Rescue workers tunnelled and blasted a path underground, while listening for any sounds from the survivors.

14

Days passed. Frightened to move, the men tried to stay hopeful that they would be found. Then they heard a voice. The telehandler had been discovered from the surface.

We're down here! We're alive!

Help us!

Rescue workers drilled a hole to the cage of the telehandler. They delivered food, water and supplies to the two men.

Finally, on 9 May after two weeks trapped underground, the two men were freed from their prison. They came up to a world eager to hear their story.

Both men agreed on one thing: Their mining careers were over. They planned to never again work underground.

CHAPTER FOUR

LI ANNING
CLASSROOM TREMORS

On 12 May 2008, 16-year-old Li Anning was among 1,000 students and teachers inside her six-storey middle school in Beichuan, China. In the middle of a geography lesson, Anning felt the building shake.

Tremors rocked Anning's fourth-floor classroom. In an instant, the entire school building collapsed.

Anning had difficulty seeing around the room after the earthquake. Then she spotted the white shirt of fellow classmate Li Yuanfeng.

Anning remembered the moment well: I grabbed one of Yuanfeng's hands, calling out to him, but he didn't respond. In the beginning, I could feel the warmth of his hand, but soon it cooled.

She called out the names of her classmates one by one. Even though she couldn't see her classmates, she could hear them. They stayed positive by singing some of their favourite songs.

Finally, after 40 hours, Anning and her classmates were saved.

After the rescue operation had concluded it was revealed that about 70,000 people died as a result of the earthquake. An estimated 18,000 remain missing to this day, which makes Anning's terrifying story even more incredible.

CHAPTER FIVE

EVANS MONSIGNAC
TRAPPED UNDER CONCRETE

Evans Monsignac, a 27-year-old father of two, was working at a marketplace in Port-au-Prince, Haiti, on 12 January 2010. It was a typical day for Monsignac, but disaster struck in a matter of moments.

As Monsignac was selling cooking oil and rice, a 7.0-magnitude earthquake shook the marketplace.

Monsignac lost his balance and fell to the ground. He was quickly pinned between two large concrete slabs.

Unable to move, he watched in horror as a third concrete slab fell towards him.

Amazingly, the other two concrete slabs protected him from being crushed.

You'll be OK. We'll get you out of here.

Monsignac was transported to a hospital in Florida, USA to recover. Doctors were amazed that despite suffering from dehydration, his kidneys were unharmed.

The earthquake's final death toll ranged from 230,000 to 316,000, but Monsignac's story jumped to the top of the headlines. He is believed to be the only person to have survived being trapped so long after an earthquake without receiving food, water or supplies from rescue workers.

CHAPTER SIX

BRIAN COKER
DISASTER AT THE OFFICE

Brian Coker was an ordinary businessman working in Christchurch, New Zealand. On 22 February 2011, he began his day by dropping off his wife, Helen, at the airport. He had no idea of the disaster that was about to strike the city.

Bye, Helen! Have a great time with your parents!

From the airport, he went in to work. At lunch time, he headed to the stairwell. That's when the earthquake hit. He hung on to the railing as ceiling tiles crashed down.

In an instant, a concrete wall shook loose and fell on top of him.

Then everything went dark.

When Coker came round, pain was shooting through his entire body.

He recalled: I knew straight away I was pinned and there was no way I could get myself out.

Within hours of her call, help arrived at the scene.

Coker knew he would have to keep his wits to survive. So he focused on breathing, even though getting air was hard. Concrete dust coated the inside of his nose and mouth.

He texted his wife and explained his situation. She called the police and told them where her husband was and what he was wearing.

Don't worry, Sir. We're going to get you out of here.

CHAPTER SEVEN

HARUMI WATANABE
WAVE OF DESTRUCTION

On 11 March 2011, a 9.0-magnitude earthquake off the coast of Japan triggered a 9-metre tall tsunami. Those in the path of this huge wave could do little but hang on and hope. Harumi Watanabe of Shintona did everything she could to save her parents, and ultimately, to survive.

At work in her small shop, Watanabe was unaware of the destruction yet to come.

RUMMMMBLE!

At 2.46 p.m. that day, the powerful earthquake struck, nearly knocking her to the floor.

The rising water soon came up to Watanabe's neck. With only a small space of air under the ceiling, she had to act quickly.

She stood on the furniture to keep her head above water.

Watanabe was only one of a few Shintona residents to survive the tsunami. While she mourned the loss of her parents, her story of survival became a message of hope after the deadly disaster.

GLOSSARY

AMPUTATE cut off someone's arm, leg or other body part

ANAESTHETIC gas or injection that prevents pain during treatments and operations

CHASM deep hole or opening in Earth's surface

CORPSE dead body

DEHYDRATION life-threatening medical condition caused by a lack of water

MAGNITUDE unit for measuring an earthquake's power

PLIGHT bad situation or state of being

SEWAGE human waste material carried away from homes by pipes

TREMOR shaking movement of the ground before or after an earthquake

TSUNAMI large, destructive wave caused by an underwater earthquake

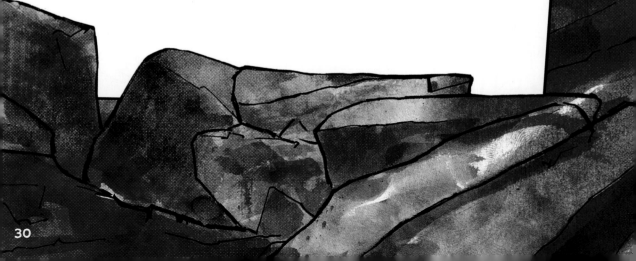

INDEX

READ MORE

Dynamic Planet: Exploring Changes on Earth with Science Projects (Discover Earth Science), Tammy Enz (Raintree, 2015)

Earthquake: Perspectives on Earthquake Disasters (Disaster Dossiers), Anne Rooney (Raintree, 2014)

Fearsome Forces of Nature (Extreme Nature), Anita Ganeri (Raintree, 2013)

Surviving Earthquakes (Children's True Stories: Natural Disasters), Kevin Cunningham (Raintree, 2012)

WEBSITES

www.ngkids.co.uk/science-and-nature/structure-of-the-earth
Learn about the structure of Earth and the science behind earthquakes.

nhm.ac.uk/nature-online/earth/volcanoes-earthquakes/earthquakes/index.html
Visit the National History Museum's website and find out more about earthquakes and tsunamis, and how scientists are working to more accurately predict earthquakes.